WELL-BEING
30 SMALL STEPS

CAROLINE REAGH

First published in Great Britain in 2023
Independent Publishing Network

Text copyright © Caroline Reagh 2023

Typesetting and cover design by Laura Kincaid
Ten Thousand | Editing + Book Design
www.tenthousand.co.uk

ISBN 9781803528823

All rights reserved. No part of this work may be reproduced or utilized in any form or by any means, electronic or mechanical, including photocopying, recording, or by any information storage and retrieval system, without the prior permission of the author.

A CIP catalogue record for this book is available from the British Library upon request

Printed by Mixam

for
Koit and Uta
precious memories

CONTENTS

	Introduction – Well-Being	2
1	Celebrate Friends and People you Love	4
2	Meditate	6
3	Smile	8
4	Wait	10
5	Connect	12
6	Walk	14
7	Sing	18
8	Eat Colour	20
9	Savour Moments	22
10	Exercise	24
11	Sit and Sit for Longer	26
12	Empty Space	28
13	Breathe	30
14	Laugh	34
15	Sleep Well	36
16	Drink	38
17	Observe Animals	42
18	Observe Thoughts	44
19	Reflect with Ease	46
20	Stretch	48
21	Write	50
22	Take Time	52
23	Create a Routine	56

24	Form Good Habits	58
25	Break a Routine	60
26	Give Thanks	64
27	Witness Magical Moments	66
28	Speak Uplifting Words	68
29	Appreciate Your Body	70
30	The Best Feeling Thought in Each Moment	72
Acknowledgements		74
Photo Credits		75
About the Author		76

WELL-BEING

A few years ago, I spent five wet winter weeks on Vancouver Island, British Columbia. The house had a fabulous library and one of my morning rituals was to read a 'thought for the day' from a beautiful book by Mark Nepo titled *The Book of Awakening*. This inspired in me a feeling of calm and a sense of focus for the day ahead. Now, having spent many months in a quiet isolated hamlet in the French Pyrenees, I have learned to create and follow many of my own small rituals. These have contributed to a greater sense of calm, clarity and well-being. As a result, my life has become progressively more enjoyable.

One morning I wrote down some of these practices and the list came to thirty. Whilst these are by no means new ideas, I would like to share my approach to each one. When I listen to a particular meditation, speak well with a friend, or truly take time to appreciate a small thing that has happened, it somehow encourages me to repeat these activities. Small repetitions of good things have the effect of realising and encouraging even more good things.

I believe that well-being can be cultivated. This is not to deny all the situations, circumstances and responsibilities in life which challenge us. Sometimes life can be concerning, uncertain and very difficult. However, practising activities that provide a sense of well-being can increase and strengthen our ability to cope with and enjoy life more.

I have dedicated many years of my life to respecting, training and guiding my body towards good physical health.

I have discovered the positive effects this has also had on the health of my mind. I was not brought up, however, with the idea of training and helping my mind to be well. It has only been in more recent years that I have been inspired to focus on what and how I think. It is well recognised that regular, consistent practice of how one focuses one's mind can bring about significant changes to our attitudes. I have learned to focus my attention on encouraging good feelings through both physical and mental activities.

So why do we need to practise this? Well, as with most things, we do it to get better at something we value and feel is worth doing. For me, increasing a sense of well-being seems worth practising, worth sharing and worth writing about. One person feels good, they share it, and a powerful chain of positive emotions gathers momentum.

The thirty practices I describe are not written in any particular order so you can choose any one of them at any time. Some may interest you more than others. Try some things that may be new to you and see if you are pleasantly surprised with the result. After reading the book from beginning to end, note what has created the best feelings for you and plan how to rediscover that on a regular basis.

CELEBRATE FRIENDS AND PEOPLE YOU LOVE

Taking part in activities with friends and loved ones is often taken for granted. Enjoying the company of good friends and sharing thoughts and feelings is what makes friendships special.

- *think back to a time or a place you enjoyed sharing with a friend or loved one, it can be very simple*

- *recreate the feelings in your mind and the details, close your eyes and savour the memory*

- *do the above with friends and loved ones from the past and present and with new friends*

- *let go of any thoughts that don't feel good, and refocus on what was enjoyable*

- *give thanks for the friendship, say it aloud, or in your mind write down a few words of what you enjoyed*

- *if you like send a short text to the friend reminding them of the time, saying what you enjoyed*

- *begin a simple journal of friend celebrations, often one or two words can jog your memory*

MEDITATE

This is something to do every day. Meditation does not have to be complicated. It is simple and there are numerous ways to practise. All it takes is an intention and focus. That's it. Remember, practise makes it easier. I have been particularly inspired by Deepak Chopra, Jon Kabat-Zinn and Sarah Raymond. They each provide many different guided meditation practices that you can find on the internet, of different lengths, to get you started. Find one you like and stay with that for a while. The more you turn up to meditate, the easier it becomes. Little and often, is a path to get most things up and running. For me, meditation is a real pleasure. Sometimes, it just takes a bit of getting used to saying, doing, and thinking, nothing in particular. I save a number of meditations from the internet on my phone, so I don't need to think about what meditation to do if I want to listen to someone.

- *sit down for just ten minutes and be quiet with your mind. If thoughts come in, let them drift by. No fighting, no struggle, just breathe. Breathe in and breathe out. If you find this difficult, start with ten breaths*

- *the next day turn up again for yourself and do the same*

SMILE

Just the word alone can make one smile inside. The word seems soft and open. If you are a visual person there are so many internal images one can hold of the word smile. I suspect these images have a visceral effect on the body and mind. When you see someone smiling, really focus on it and try memorising the image. Allow yourself to really enjoy that smile. I sometimes do this when I recall a conversation and find it lightens the way I feel. The joy of seeing others smile can have a considerable effect on your well-being. There is something very honest and beautiful about a smile that lights up a face. It is to be treasured.

> *spend ten seconds frowning and focus on how that feels in the body*

> *spend ten seconds smiling and focus on how that feels in the body*

- *do the same but think of the smile as being inside the body in your stomach area*

- *then imagine the frown being inside the body in the stomach area, how does that make you feel?*

- *does it make you want to consider carrying a smile around inside you?*

- *play around with putting the smile in or on different body parts*

WAIT

When we wish things to happen, we often take action and have an expectation of when we want the result. Learning to wait or pause in our lives allows us to feel a sense of ease. Waiting gives time and space, so there is a natural opening, an empty place. These empty places are important. They are like breaths and can quietly allow life to gently unfold. So, in waiting, you let go of any need to push or force. You simply stay where you are. When we are action-oriented, this can be difficult and sometimes frustrating. But you could call waiting an action, as it is in music. The spaces and silence can increase the beauty and intensity of what has gone before and what is coming next. Also, inspiration can arrive in the wait.

> *wait for something you have taken action towards with light expectation*

- *pause more often between activities, even for just a minute or two*

- *sit still, looking, with no expectation*

- *sit still, listening, with no expectation*

- *sit still, feeling the air around your body, with no expectation*

CONNECT

Taking time to contact family and friends you know well, and also people you don't know so well often brings positive feelings. Regardless of the outcome, you have taken a decision to reach out. You never know how other people really feel and what effect you are having. So, if you approach the person with what you can give, that intention alone serves you well. Appreciating all the small things that make people tick and give them a reason to be cheerful is something to notice and enjoy oneself. Perhaps one can be surprised or delighted to share what makes someone else happy. Comforting a family member, friend or even someone unknown is special. This doesn't mean 'fixing' anything about the other person. Simply caring to listen is good for the talker and the listener. Being of help, even if the help is small, creates good feelings, so keep the focus on that.

- *arrange to have a phone call with someone at an arranged time, convenient for both of you*

- *send a text to someone, even if months or years have passed since you last did this*

- *send an email focusing on the receiver rather than listing your own activities*

- *write a letter, or card or send a postcard, even if you live close by*

- *arrange to meet and do something that pleases both parties*

- *volunteer, choose something that interests you and search the internet for volunteer opportunities that closely match that*

WALK

I walk by myself twice each day accompanied by our dog. This is a good time to concentrate and sense, in detail, the surroundings. When I remember, I prompt myself to observe my thoughts, yet refrain from engaging in them. Mostly, I walk with the intention to observe. This observation can be inner or outer and often fluctuates between the two. Walking, without thinking of the destination and without thinking about what to do next or considering life's specific challenges is freeing. Everything can be put on pause. Of course, thoughts come and go but the act of walking can make it easier to let things fall away. The thoughts are 'on the move', through the act of walking. And this movement can bring shifts in perspective. Try walking with the focus and intention to do each of the following separately for at least ten minutes.

> *SEE really look with full focus and concentration at what is all around you, underneath, beside, and above you. Look at your immediate vicinity and also far away. Sometimes stop to look at something that takes your attention*

> *HEAR practise the same as above but listening*

> *FEEL are you hot, cold, or just the right temperature? Focus on different parts of the body from the feet up to the head. How do they feel? Do this without judgement or the thought to fix anything, simply observe. Where can you feel the air on your body? What are your emotional feelings? Do they change from the beginning of the walk to the end? It's always easiest to begin focusing on the senses with your own immediate body responses*

> *SMELL what can you smell? Coffee from a thermos? A flower? An animal? Clothing? Play a game to count different smells over ten minutes*

> *TASTE depending on where you walk, there may be little to taste. If in natural surroundings outdoors, try sampling one of a few pieces of vegetation you know to be safe. Picnics of course have many tastes, savour every mouthful on your next outdoor picnic. Imagine tastes*

SING

When we think of singing for ourselves, the tendency is to think of choirs or groups. The song 'Stand by Me' has been running through my head for a few days. It occurs to me that, this song, mostly sung about someone else standing by me, could so easily be about me standing by me. That's the great thing about songs and singing, you can be taken anywhere. The words can bring back memories, project you to a future and hold or reflect you in the present time. Then there's the singing and notes arranged to become the song, the melody, the tune, the passage to a new place.

> ➢ *hum or sing a few notes, start with two notes for a few minutes then add a third*

> ➢ *play around with the above, maybe you get bored, or maybe you just enjoy singing a few notes, that's all*

- *try singing, loud, quiet, gentle, harsh, classical, rock, opera-style, or any style*

- *find a favourite song, learn one verse then see what happens*

- *sing your favourite nursery rhyme then randomly join it to other nursery rhymes until you have five or six!*

- *sing the same song for a week or a month until you know it with or without music accompaniment*

- *commit to ten minutes of singing a day for a week and observe how that makes you feel*

- *or even just listen to the same song every day for a week*

When you concentrate on the words of a song or try to remember the notes, it is then quite challenging to think about anything else. You are 'taken over' by the song. The music is in you. You are breathing, and naturally shifting energy. Allowing energy to shift, means emotions and feelings can change, so you are not holding onto a particular emotional state. There is purity or clarity in the song. Words, emotions, notes, breath, voice and body all focused on the song. Find one you like and take pleasure and enjoyment from it.

EAT COLOUR

Three shades of green, with orange, yellow, pink and white. Just finished lunch. I could have added purple, red and brown but seven colours on the plate were enough for now. Bright food colours tend to come from a range of vegetables and fruit unless using food colourings which I would not really recommend. Eating plenty of vegetables and fruit provides lots of minerals, micronutrients and antioxidants to the cells of the body. These all help your body to function optimally. The more colour you eat the healthier the body can be. The longer a vegetable is cooked, the paler it becomes. Overcooking, unless slowly at a low temperature with all the liquid retained, reduces the vitality transferred from the vegetable to you.

> *try eating eight different food colours a day*

> *have four colours in a meal, you don't have to eat it all together. The French eat almost one ingredient at a time. The small pauses between courses are so good for the digestion*

> *grow and eat nasturtium flowers, they are great in salads, quite piquant*

> *eat as much green as possible, the darker the better, broccoli, spinach, chard, kale, and home-sprouted grains are full of vitamin B12, great for energy*

> *find vibrant colours to eat, enjoy the colourful choices presented in food markets and supermarkets, use only a small percentage of white*

White foods like white bread, sugar, rice and potatoes are simply not as nutritious as brighter coloured food. The saying 'you are what you eat' holds some truth. I believe the food and drink you put in your mouth (and possibly more importantly the thoughts you put in your mind) have an enormous and powerful effect on how you feel. How you feel, is how you are in the world. Are you how you want to be? If not, begin making small changes to what you eat and what you think.

SAVOUR MOMENTS

Anything that helps savour a moment adds to the enjoyment of life. There is always something to savour.

   sun shining on a stone wall
                    leaves rustling in the wind
                            washing, drying outside on a line
             dogs lounging in the sun
 the sip of a soothing drink
                    a comfortable chair
   shared time with good friends
                          sea lapping on a pebble beach

Moments passing, moments fleeting, although short-lived can add up to a huge bank of beautiful memories. Moment, after moment, after moment creates a life, so I like to remember to bring attention to them. It feels good to fully attend with all one's senses to the nuances of the moment. Writing this, memories from the past drift into mind. So, it's two for one! You savour it at the time and again as a future memory. This is really a slow, mindful appreciation of life. Sometimes, it's almost like 'coasting', taking your foot off the accelerator pedal and observing. There is no striving, no driving action forward and no pushing. It's almost like taking a breath in, pausing and then letting it out slowly. The pause and the slow breath out allows you the time to savour what is going on.

> *look around you now and savour what is there*

> *list some of your own savoured moments*

EXERCISE

I cannot imagine a life without exercise. So, if you find exercise a chore, forgive me, as I am a convert. I do not need to report on the massive benefits exercise has on our physical and mental health. There seems to be no controversy on that. However, if you find it hard to do any exercise I can understand. Where to start? I think a good place is with your mind. Try answering these questions.

> ***why do I want to** exercise?*

> ***what** shall I do?*

Walk, cycle, run, swim, go to the gym, do yoga, find a cardio workout, jump on a mini trampoline, skip, dance, use a hula hoop… and the list goes on. Find something, anything, to start with. So here are the next questions.

➢ ***when*** *will I do my exercise?*

➢ ***why*** *exercise?*

For me, it really is an appointment in my diary and I commit myself to keep that appointment. So why not put it in your diary?

➢ ***how long*** *will my exercise session be?*

If you are just starting out, I would suggest ten minutes. A commitment to practise sets you up for the day or punctuates the day with positive intent. Ten minutes every day for four or five days each week and you are off!

For those people who regularly exercise, try adding or replacing one or two of your sessions with something new. If you always stretch, try light weights, or vice versa. Varying a routine now and again, strengthens and stretches different muscles in the body and can inspire you and feel refreshing.

So, begin. You will feel better because you have committed to yourself, you will benefit physically and mentally, and your confidence will increase as you become more proficient. To begin with, you may not feel like jumping for joy. However, if you focus clearly and decisively on a positive, enjoyable activity for you, this in time will make you feel good.

SIT AND SIT FOR LONGER

Some people cannot sit still at all. When we sit, there is a tendency to also be doing something, watching television, eating, working, reading, and creating. Sitting still can allow the mind and body to settle. After a while, the chatter of the mind drifts away or takes you somewhere else. An idea comes, and then another. Sitting still with the body and mind can allow thoughts to come and go. Like a butterfly landing on a flower or plant, it has no need to linger for long in any one place. Let yourself do this with no expectations. Allow thoughts and feelings to flutter by, not becoming attached to any one thing. Eventually, everything slows down, breathing, thoughts, and sensory observations. This gives the opportunity to take in more, almost expanding the mind as you quieten. You, sitting there in the world, letting things be, with a quiet curiosity. That is all.

- *for now, accept an invitation to simply sit down in a comfortable place, inside or outside, with nothing to do except sit and observe*

- *simply let yourself be sitting, with no particular intention*

- *allow a softness, a gentle awareness to arise*

EMPTY SPACE

Where is the space in your life? There can be space in your mind, body, home, garden, travelling place, workspace, diary and more. In all of these, there can be space or clutter or somewhere in between the two. As we move through life we collect experiences, ideas, beliefs, and 'things'. We collect, acquire and over time fill our lives with 'things'. Some of these are precious, hold memories and provide joy, comfort and security. Sometimes there is a tipping point and we clear cupboards, clothes, shelves, and rooms, in order to reflect, reorganise and keep what we feel we need. The home seems to be central to clearing, like a bird cleaning a nest from the previous year. More challenging is clearing space in your daily routines and probably the biggest challenge is emptying space in your mind or clearing out ideas and beliefs that no longer serve you. Doing this can help you feel in control, allow you to function with more ease, give you more free time, feel clear and open, allow new ideas to enter and feel refreshing. How do you know a belief or idea needs clearing? The easiest way is to tell from how you feel. Is it comfortable, easy, flowing, expansive, open, or has potential? If it is none of those then let it go.

- *look at the different aspects of your life. Where can you clear, make space, or drop something? or what can you do less often?*

- *start small, maybe clear a drawer in a room, or clear a day or a week in your diary*

- *decide on a timescale, an hour, a day, a week, or a month of making space*

- *try considering your beliefs once a day for a week, and write your thoughts in a journal*

BREATHE

All day long we do it and all night too. Ninety percent of the time or more, most of us are not even aware of our breath and yet without it, we would not exist. As soon as someone mentions it or I read about it, I immediately note how I am breathing. So, writing this, I have become aware of my breath. Is it deep, or shallow, where do I feel it? So, stop now and take five deep breaths, pausing between the in-breath and the out-breath and then also pausing after the out-breath. Then go back to your normal breathing. Doing just that can be calming. For me, breath and breathing techniques are fascinating. Yogis, meditators, mental health specialists, medical practitioners, singers, dancers, athletes and many other groups and individuals pay special attention to and recognise the power of the breath. Breathing well, affects every aspect of our being, assisting the function of all our internal organs. I once read the breath out was more important than the breath in. Perhaps it is because we focus less on breathing out. You cannot fill a cup with fresh water unless it is empty. Breathing well can refresh, cleanse, calm, enliven, focus, relax, soften, regenerate, inspire (literally!), recreate and more.

> *breathe in for four, hold for four, breathe out for four, and pause for four. Eventually, increase to six or eight counts or stay with the four counts and do this for five or ten minutes*

> *alternative nostril breathing: place the first two fingers of your right hand between your eyebrows, breathe out, place your right ring finger over the left nostril, breathe in through the right nostril for four counts, place your right thumb over the right nostril, hold for eight, open the left nostril and breathe out for four, pause for four, breathe in through the left nostril for four, close, hold for eight, open the right nostril, breathe out for four, repeat for a few minutes*

> *lie on your back, place one hand gently on your stomach, breathe in and let the stomach rise up, breathe out and let it drop down, place your hand on your chest and do the same, relax your arms by your sides, take your focus to different body parts imagining sending the breath there*

> *explore the numerous breathing techniques you can find on the internet, it is easier to listen and do rather than read and do*

> *three times a day, become aware of your breath, take five deep breaths and move on*

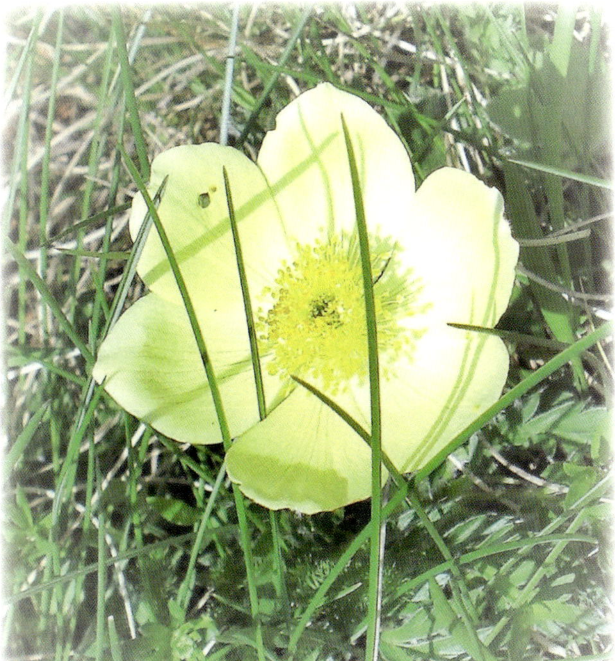

LAUGH

'… and the whole world laughs with you,' was written over one hundred years ago by American poet and journalist Ella Wheeler Wilcox. Laughing is contagious and has many benefits. It ignites positive interactions with others, can strengthen your immune system, increase blood flow, improve your mood, lessen pain in the mind and body and protect you from stress. It can inspire hope, allow you to let go of and overcome problems, add joy to your life, enhance your relationships, trigger the body's natural feel-good chemicals and help you relax. Laughter really is a medicine when you list all of these benefits. Doctors, neuroscientists and psychologists have all studied and written about the benefits of laughter.

Perhaps one needs to dedicate a bit of time to focus on laughter. It seems odd to do that, and perhaps reading this you feel you laugh a lot already. Great, but if you don't, it is just like practising any other activity, emotion, or habit that you wish to increase in your life. We easily follow our habitual behaviour. If we wish to improve and enjoy our lives more it requires focusing attention. Yes, even to laugh more.

- *begin with a smile, it's just physically turning up the sides of your mouth, then letting the whole face join in*

- *smile at yourself in the mirror every day for a week for about ten seconds, I know, it feels stupid, so what*

- *create a playlist of four funny films and watch one every two weeks*

- *find a comedian you like or a comedy programme or video and commit to watching it at least once a week for six weeks. It can be a short clip of a few minutes. You will get hooked and then remember what you watched and share it with others and laugh again*

- *display in a prominent place, some photos of yourself, family, and friends having fun*

- *for two weeks try to either find something each day that makes you laugh or do something that amuses you, play*

SLEEP WELL

Everyone's sleep pattern is different. And we all remember a fabulous well-rested, relaxed sleep we have had. There are so many ways to stall having good sleeping habits. We can remember how challenging our days are without a night of good sleep but rarely give credit to a fabulous slumber having created a great day. There are many benefits to a good night's sleep.

boosts the immune system
improves mood by reducing stress on the mind and body
increases productivity because you have more energy
helps your memory
helps control metabolism and weight
restores and rejuvenates all parts of the body and mind
helps you to function at your best
sleep heals

The general consensus seems to be that seven to eight hours of sleep a night is best for optimal function.

- *create a bedtime routine, so find a way to 'wind down' before bed, this is important as it helps set the body clock to know when to 'switch off'*

- *reduce blue light from computers and phones at least an hour before bed, read a book instead*

- *avoid alcohol before bed, and drink before 8pm*

- *try to sleep and wake at the same times*

- *increase time spent in natural light during the day*

- *try a magnesium supplement to help relaxation and improve sleep*

- *take a warm relaxing bath or shower*

- *ensure your bedroom is not too warm, a complete blackout in the room is most beneficial and also allow for some air circulation*

- *drift off to sleep listening to a meditation*

DRINK

I write this over a cup of coffee. I also regularly drink Earl Grey tea, herbal tea, water, sparkling water, and rarely, if ever, bought juice, sometimes my own pressed juices, more in the summer and yes alcohol too. During and after completing a Nutritional Healing course I was a habitual drinker of two litres of water a day. This increase in drinking water was a hugely significant and important change for me. Yes, I went to the toilet more, but yes too, my skin became clearer, my mind sharper, I had far fewer afternoon slumps of energy and I never again had another headache until I had an injury.

Our bodies are sixty percent water and our brains are eighty percent. Visualise the plants in your garden without water, the same happens to your body and brain, they shrivel up and hang on! Some studies have shown that it takes two litres of water simply for our body to do what it needs to do in a day. To function well, our cells need to communicate, and the body needs to digest and process all our daily activities both mental and physical. Initially, the more I drank, the more I recognised my thirst. This eventually balanced out. I was also careful to increase my Omega 3 oil intake. Oil and water are needed together as they affect the functioning of all the cells in the body. Fifty to sixty percent of our cell membranes are oil. After about three years I became less disciplined in my water consumption. Many of us are unknowingly in a state of constant dehydration. Now I remind myself to drink water daily and adopt the following techniques to inspire me when I feel a little nudge to drink more.

- *have an attractive water bottle that you like and can carry with you if out for the day*

- *place a lovely glass bottle or jug full of water on the kitchen table to encourage regular intake throughout the day*

- *in winter take the chill off the water by adding some hot*

- *add slices of lemon, orange, lime or mint*

- *choose a favourite glass to drink from*

- *savour the taste, acknowledging that it is nourishment*

- *remind yourself how plants shrivel without water and how they blossom and shine with it*

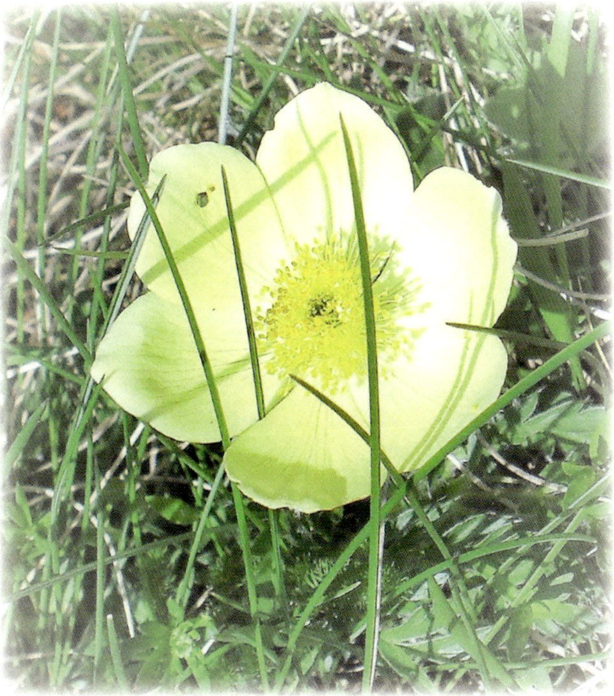

OBSERVE ANIMALS

Are there any horses, dogs, cats, donkeys, goats, pigs, sheep, or other animals around you? Include birds, insects, or whatever takes your interest, and really observe them with all your senses. Because they cannot talk, one is invited to find a different way to observe, communicate or connect with an animal. It is quite easy with a pet as they tend to be with you for a number of years. Sometimes just observing from a distance is intriguing, with no need to interact. Their world is not ours. Somehow, wind, water, air, sun, and habitat have a more immediate and direct effect on animals. They are many steps closer to the natural environment. Watching them can provide hours of delight. It's just the looking, and then a feeling arises from inside that looking. It can be fear, excitement, calm, pleasure, joy, wonder, and more. The following moments that I have witnessed have provided me with all of the above energising feelings.

    horses preening each other
        my dog careering into the woods on her own trail
  a hedgehog rising up to reveal its long legs to run across the garden
      a bear slowly disappearing into the morning mist on a riverbank
                dolphins leaping and playing, racing along at the bow of the boat
    vultures playing in wind corridors near mountain tops
        winter hares 'skeltering' through the snow
the same spider crawling down the settee three days in a row, when I started to dance
        a snake sunning itself in the undergrowth
  my old cat crossing the wet grass to join me on the garden bench

> ➢ *over the next week take your focus to an animal, bird, or insect. Suspend any preconceptions, just observe with all your senses. How does it make you feel?*

OBSERVE THOUGHTS

Observe your thoughts without becoming fully involved in them. Take a step back, imagine you are the onlooker. It doesn't take much to do this. Just a little space or breath after your observation gives the possibility of awareness. This also affords time to choose how to react or even not to react. Like anything, it takes a bit of practice. The more you can observe your thoughts, and become aware of them, the less control they have over you. More importantly, you have more control over them. Ask yourself honestly, how often are you controlled by your thoughts? Or vice versa. In a world where there are many influences, friends, family, environment, work, health and activities, all requiring attention, we tend to arrange our time to dedicate to each of these. Yet our thoughts often miss out on this dedicated time, they are just there, popping into our heads all the time.

Well, that's me you say, they are my thoughts, I own them, I created them. Are you sure? Are you really sure? Many thoughts are generated by one's upbringing, life experiences, environment and social groups. After observing one of your thoughts, ask questions: is it true? is it serving me? is it helpful? does it make me feel good? If the answer is no, then the thought needs to change or be replaced.

Is there a point in having unhelpful thoughts? They can help you recognise something is not right and when that is acknowledged you can begin to take steps towards thoughts that better serve you. It is not to push the thought away, bury it, or stamp it to the ground.

> *observe a thought and take time to really acknowledge it. Then give it some space, be gentle and allow it to be there. Perhaps even thank it and if you wish to, if it no longer serves you, let it go*

> *another approach is to let the mind do its own thing, allow it to turn things round and round but don't give it your power or focus, attend to something else which pleases you*

REFLECT WITH EASE

Even the word ease is enjoyable. It conjures up images of relaxation, softness, gentle feelings and unhurried activities. It almost invites breath, particularly exhalation where one can let go, open, and allow space. To reflect with ease is to allow contemplation without too much judgement or weighted consideration. A reflection is something mirrored back to you. Insight can spring from ease, another way of seeing 'into' a situation, an accurate and deep understanding. Reflecting with ease means there is no tension, neither in body nor mind. Easily, one can let thoughts come and go. Allow them to dissolve and melt away or hold them gently in a fluid form. Not rushing or forcing reflection to come but waiting, even daydreaming.

> *sit and watch the cloudscape for a few moments*

- *listen to your breath and attend to where it is moving in your body*

- *scan your body from head to toe, inviting a release of any tension, then repeat this for a second time*

- *dilly-dally for a bit, somewhere new, just dilly-dally*

- *truly focus on ease, in the body, at different times of the day*

- *expect things to be easy, or to happen with a flow*

- *be at ease, reflect with ease*

STRETCH

To stretch is to lengthen, pull out, or elongate. Think of a medical skeleton and the bones dangling, then dress the bones with fascia, tendons and muscles. All of the latter, without an underlying health condition, permit the mechanical structure of the body to stand without too much muscle contraction.

> ➢ *try standing now, and scan the body from the feet up. Just for a moment take your attention to your feet, ankles, knees, hips, waist, shoulders, arms, wrists, hands, neck, head, jaw, and face. Often, simply taking attention to an area of the body can release tension*

The above can be a preparation to stretch. Why stretch? Skeletal muscles are designed to contract and relax, to mechanically move the body. If a muscle works hard in contraction without being relaxed, its elasticity is weakened and becomes less efficient. We contract many muscles on a daily basis with repetitive tasks such as driving, making the bed, washing dishes, sitting at a desk or in a chair, and lifting and storing shopping. Walking can stretch us out through the process of folding and unfolding joints, breathing, and allowing the arms to hang naturally. Although advised to move around hourly when working on a computer, who actually does this? Do you? Stretching does not have to involve yoga or specific athletic positions. To lengthen, pull out or elongate parts of the body can be done anywhere, anytime. Even lengthening the spine whilst seated at a table to eat, encourages a stretch. Stretching offers space, enabling joints to function well. Stretching around the diaphragm, taking deep breaths focussed around the rib cage, also allows the internal organs to regulate and function more easily.

> ➢ *this week, try a daily two to five-minute stretch, standing, seated, or lying down. Begin gently, stretching any part of the body your attention is taken to*

WRITE

Anything can be written, thoughts, dreams, plans, feelings. Sometimes one word can be placed on a page and others follow. It is another way to bring thoughts and feelings to the surface. This can be interesting to reflect on. Some people write a daily journal finding satisfaction from the process. Others have a gratitude book, writing thanks for what they have.

- *put pen or pencil to paper and just write anything down, a free flow of anything, and keep going for two or three pages. Do this daily for a week or two and see if any patterns arise or potential solutions to challenges you may have or insights into situations. This approach is best done with no expectations. Expecting a solution can block the flow. Allow the words to come*

- *try a gratitude diary, writing down three things you are grateful for each day, in any aspect of your life.*

See how it makes you feel after a week or so. The act of writing what you are grateful for gives it extra acknowledgement, providing additional satisfaction

- *try writing a letter to a friend, a description of your day, an observation of your pet, or someone else's, a view from a window, some favourite words and string them together in a sentence, a short story for a child, an adventure you would like to have*

These are all for fun, for your enjoyment. Try it and see what shows up on the page. You might surprise yourself.

TAKE TIME

We are encouraged to use our time wisely and not waste it. This can cause us to over-structure our day and become frustrated when our 'to-do' list is not shortened. Or our days can be too full with little time for reflection or pause, causing tension and stress. Perhaps we can redefine for ourselves what we wish to do with our time.

> *take time to do something you enjoy each day, week, month, and each year*

What might these things be? Commit them to your diary, make the appointment and turn up. If life gets in the way, just try again until the appointments become easier to keep. Monthly and annual commitments can be even more special, different, or new. Experiment with new ideas. Have no concern about how your ideas can happen. For now, just take time to daydream. The possibility and reality of manifesting these daydreams can be considered at a later date. Even just daydreaming creates good feelings, worth taking time for.

> *take time to be completely engaged in what you are doing*

Empty your head of what needs to be done and what you will do next, simply be here in this moment. To do this, bring awareness to your body, how does it feel? Or pay attention to the breath. Is it fast, deep, or shallow? Where is the breath?

> *take all the time you need to do what you are doing*

Imagine there is no rush, that there is all the time in the world. There can be little moments of observation when you take your time. When one says to a child, 'take your time', it invites them to take a breath, feel at ease and concentrate on their activity. Time marches on and waits for no one, it is said. Time is divided, programmed and used in our days. This can be self-motivated or externally controlled or a bit of both.

> *occasionally it may be good to wake up and decide to have no plans for the day. Let the day unfold, so to speak, with your own inspirations. Listen to your intuition and guidance before taking any action*

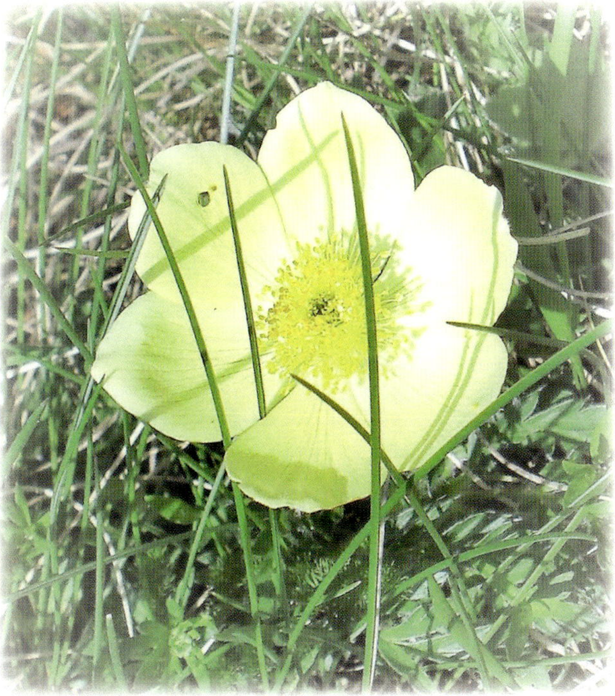

CREATE A ROUTINE

Routines can feel satisfying and productive. When some parts of your day flow along with the same regular activities they can happen quite easily. You don't have to introduce an idea, plan what is required, and then do it, because it just falls into place through habit. Knowing you meditate every morning, means you probably know where, when, what time, what you will be wearing and when you may finish. This generally happens, for most pre-planned routine activities. Adding something new to your routine does require thought and commitment, but it definitely becomes easier. Perhaps not all of our days or every day has a routine we particularly like. We can always find ways to improve our routines or adjust them for our benefit, helping us to feel better, and more in control. It is good if some of your routines can be either, satisfying, fulfilling, enriching, nourishing, or all of the above. How great is it to have parts of your day you completely and utterly enjoy or even all of your day? Below are some routines you can try. All of these are simple and require little time. Savour, build and enjoy the routines you create. Then change or tweak them periodically.

- *light candles at a certain time of day*

- *drink a glass of water every morning and afternoon*

- *meditate daily at a certain time*

- *take a shower or bath before bed*

- *sit for five or ten minutes before dinner*

- *make the bed well before bed-time to enjoy just lying down when the time comes*

- *buy flowers for yourself*

- *take five minutes to clear or clean a space*

- *look at the sky for a few moments*

- *add anything that improves how you feel*

FORM GOOD HABITS

Good habits can be small actions, thoughts, feelings, and words that nourish you and help you thrive. Here are some that you can try.

- *speak kindly to yourself and others*
- *enjoy some early nights*
- *smile*
- *breathe deeply often*
- *eat well and not too much*
- *drink water*
- *enjoy wine and not too much*
- *clear some clutter*

> *make appointments with exercise*

> *spend time outside*

> *stare at nature sometimes*

The list goes on and wants to be made by you, for you.

> *think now of three new habits you would like to have or develop*

Commit to following one for a week and reflect on how you feel. Decide on what, where, when and how. This decision process will help make it stick. Gradually add more habits that make you feel good. Start small and appreciate each time you complete one of your habits. Remember, they are for you, not against you, so support and be gentle with yourself to help make them happen. They can be waymarks on the road, helping you to experience enjoyable days. Good habits can improve your state of mind and this carries over into other parts of your day. Achieving small tasks that you set for yourself is enjoyable, so if necessary, find creative ways to do this. Remember the habits you want to form are pulling you towards where you want to be. They can change and evolve over time. Firstly, decide on a habit to form, the reasons why, then practice.

BREAK A ROUTINE

Earlier I wrote, create a routine. Now, is it worth considering breaking a routine? Sometimes a small shift or tweak to a routine can throw up new ideas or inspiration. Try some of the following suggestions.

> *sit on a different chair for breakfast*

> *slightly alter the route of your regular walk*

> *drive or cycle a new route*

- *cook a new recipe*

- *tune into a different radio station for ten minutes*

- *call someone you know out of the blue*

- *exercise at a different time of the day*

- *stop and breathe for five minutes before beginning a new task*

- *spend longer than you planned on a particular task or do the opposite*

- *change your meal pattern, perhaps a longer, later lunch or a late breakfast*

- *buy and read a different type of magazine than you normally do*

- *take a nap*

- *go for the same walk you normally do but really look to find something new or different in the walk. Intend to find something and you will*

Changing a routine can be refreshing. Just like a holiday, the mind somehow has more space. Being in a different place takes us a step out of ourselves. We take in new experiences with our senses, so the old or patterned experiences are paused for a bit. It is like a refresh, or re-set of our default behaviour. This can allow new perspectives of our thoughts and beliefs. It seems a good idea to occasionally break our routines. We can then have more information on what routines we enjoy or not. Little by little we can consistently move towards creating daily patterns in our lives which we enjoy.

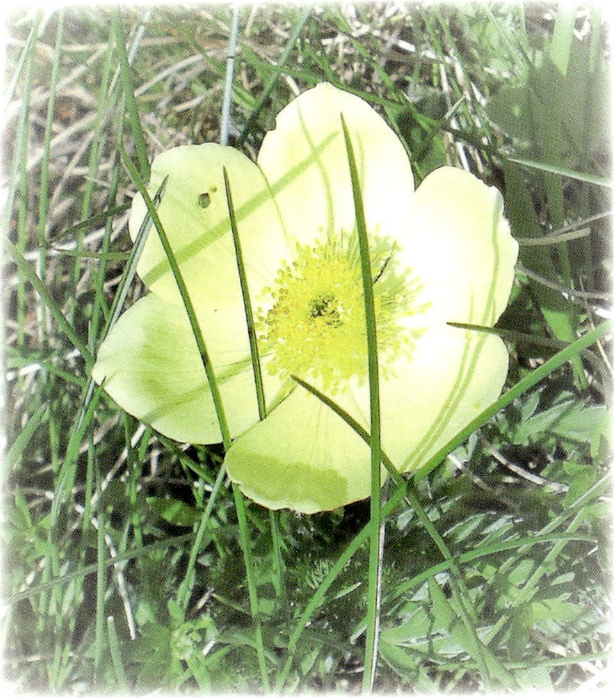

GIVE THANKS

People, places, experiences, sensations, views, the sun, the moon, and anything you can taste, see, touch, hear, or smell can be thanked. Appreciation sometimes needs a little reminder.

- *instead of focusing on something that is missing, focus on what you have and appreciate that*

- *appreciate something you expect to happen, there is always something to be grateful for*

- *try for a day, catching yourself when about to complain or worry, and replace it with thinking about something you are grateful for*

The more you practise this, the easier it becomes. This does not mean ignoring something of real concern. It is simply to notice if you more easily tend to complain or worry than give thanks and appreciation for what you have. Feeling appreciation is powerful. It promotes a physical and emotional reaction in your body and mind that feels good and can reduce stress and anxiety. Try ranting for about two minutes about what you really love or like. Say it out loud, write it, repeat it, and add to it daily. Use it as a tool when you feel upset or frustrated. Here is an introduction to a thank-you rant. I am so grateful for, the yellow flowers, my loving dog, my breath, my heart beating, the singing birds, pencils, ice in the freezer, clear windows, my comfortable car, marmalade, laughing children, butter. Just say anything that you are grateful for, there is so much to appreciate.

WITNESS MAGICAL MOMENTS

Taking the time to witness magical moments at the time they happen is important. And when you recall them they can give great pleasure again. This is so for me when I remember the following experiences.

morning mist rolling over the hillside
                                     changing shapes of clouds
    a child's delight noticing the first bat at dusk
the sensation of a ladybird walking on your hand
                hearing the first spring frogs as daylight fades
    seeing a mouse nibble a fresh green leaf
                      the dash of a squirrel passing close by
    waves lapping on a pebble beach in hot sunshine
        dolphins playing around a sailing boat
turning skis gently in light powder snow

There are so many magical moments to cherish. Sometimes we just need to focus, be open to, or expect that they will happen. The moments listed above involve the senses of touch, sight and sound. So now I might take time to recall magical moments of taste and smell. This is fun to do and can give insight into your interests, personality and character.

- ➢ *write at least five magical moments you have witnessed in your life and bask in the sensations of them*

- ➢ *what senses are prevalent in those moments?*

- ➢ *perhaps try to engage all the senses in a few magical moments?*

- ➢ *today choose one of the five senses you use less and expect a magical moment to happen with that sense*

SPEAK UPLIFTING WORDS

Abundant, beautiful, comforting, delightful, excellent, fabulous, gorgeous, happy, ignited, joyful, knowing, luxurious, magnificent, natural, opulent, perfect, quality, revelling, superb, treasured, uplifting, vibrant, wonderful, Xanadu, yes, zen. This is a little game I came across whilst listening to a meditation one day. You create the most uplifting, positive words you can, going through the alphabet. This exercise is a good one to return to and an easy way to lift one's mood. The words themselves conjure positive feelings and emotions.

> *do this yourself. Then take one word and find more uplifting words from the letters of that word. It is interesting to note what words come immediately to mind. Are they generally positive or negative? Why? Find words you like*

Receiving compliments is encouraging. Giving compliments can do the same and help you feel good. Like gifts, both giving and receiving are enjoyable. Consider the words you use when speaking to yourself and other people. Take time to reflect on this and practise, for a few days, using words that are uplifting. They don't have to be exaggerated like those above. Consider words that are kind, gentle, appreciative, generous and inspiring to yourself and others. Play around with increasing your use of uplifting words.

APPRECIATE YOUR BODY

Begin from the toes up or the head down. Take a bit of time to reflect on what different parts of your body enable you to do. Toes can wiggle in the sand, and your feet provide a platform of support for the entire body. Ankles make constant fine adjustments of balance as you move. The lower leg powers the foot and ankle with a strong calf muscle. Knees allow you to bend to the level of a child's eyes. The thighs enable you to run, jump, climb, swim, and so it continues, the wonders of our body. We expect it to work and when something goes wrong it has a big impact on how we feel and what we can do.

> *do you ever take time to really appreciate your body?*

> *what does that mean for you?*

We often think to appreciate our body means a relaxing bath or a massage or to exercise, stretch, strengthen and sleep. All of these are good and very beneficial if practiced regularly. Perhaps one can go a little deeper to appreciate and care for our bodies. Breathing in and out whilst focusing on a place in or of the body allows tension to release. Relaxing the small muscles around the face, eyes and mouth make it easier for larger muscles to let go. Consider the food, drink and thoughts your body ingests. What additional support can you give your body in these areas? The internal organs do an amazing job for you, sorting, sifting, arranging, connecting, firing, cleansing, moving and much more. Are the following images useful?

> *soften your stomach*

> *hold your heart with care*

> *laugh with your lungs*

> *spin with your spine*

> *inspire your intestine*

> *love your liver*

> *brighten your brain*

These are some ways to take your focus light-heartedly around the body and notice where and what you could appreciate more.

THE BEST FEELING THOUGHT IN EACH MOMENT

I learned to focus on the best feeling thought described by the author and inspirational speaker Esther Hicks. It is a very useful practice in many situations. You consider the thought that provides you with the best feeling you can have in any given moment. What if everything is going wrong, there's a disaster, a tragedy, anxiety, discord, or any other number of things to upset you? Yes, it is difficult and very challenging to find the best feeling thought in these times. It is not, however, impossible. Begin practising this when you feel good. Recognise a good feeling and store it somewhere in your mind or body. This will help you acknowledge and re-create it. Focus on the senses and find something that feels good when you think of it. It does not have to be happening right now. It is you who thinks your thoughts. If a thought you have makes you feel bad, find a different thought.

> *for now, write down five thoughts that make you feel good*

> *when you practise this gently with a soft heart it can become easier to do*

> *during the course of a week take a pause each day to focus on the best feeling thought at that moment*

This is not something anyone ever encouraged me to do at any stage in my life. To be thankful and grateful for what one has is similar but different. To actively choose to feel the best you can in each moment begins to pull you towards that way of thinking. It is an intention and focus that can help you feel better, lift your mood and provide more enjoyment in your days. It does not deny or ignore bad feelings. It is an awakening and a recognition of feelings and then deciding which are of most benefit.

ACKNOWLEDGEMENTS

I am so grateful to all the people and places that have inspired me to reach the point of writing this book. I am encouraged always by my close family and so many of my very good friends, through sharing honest conversations from the heart, memorable and inspiring activities, good food, wine, laughter and cups of tea. I appreciate and thank you all so very much, Alpha, Ance, Bernadette, Bobby, Chantal, Emma, Fin, Frank, Heather, Izzie, Karen, Ken, Mary, Mats, Natasha, Ron, Rosalyn, Sandra, Sheila, Susan and the many wonderful creative dancers, actors, singers, musicians and artists that I have had the great pleasure to work with. Thank you to Barry for his gentle, consistent, guiding support and constant encouragement, and his incisive comments in helping to edit this book. Thank you to everyone featured in the photos including Audrey, Frances, Hamish, John, Merryn, Ola and Sue. Card design p.12 by www.hannahlongmuir.co.uk

PHOTO CREDITS

All photographs by the author except:

Appreciate Your Body	Sandra Robertson
Sit and Sit for Longer	Barry Smith
Breathe	Emma Benbow

ABOUT THE AUTHOR

Caroline Reagh has worked as a dance artist, performer and teacher for over 40 years. She has lived in Scotland, Canada and France, where she has spent and continues to spend many hours outdoors, walking, hiking, sailing, skiing, and cycling. Her experiences of and passion for health and well-being has led to this, her first book. Caroline has also made a short dance film influenced by the ideas in the book.

YouTube: Caroline Reagh @carolinereagh650